"I knew that if I failed I wouldn't regret that, but I knew the one thing I might regret is not trying."

-Jeff Bezos

Table of Contents

Introduction

The idea of becoming a millionaire through passive income streams is an attractive one for many people. The idea of earning money without having to work for it is appealing, and the potential for financial freedom and security is a significant motivator. However, becoming a millionaire through passive income streams is not easy and requires a significant amount of determination, planning and effort.

The key to becoming a millionaire through passive income is to invest in a diversified portfolio of income streams. This means investing in a variety of different types of passive income, such as rental properties, investments, and online businesses. Diversifying one's income streams can help mitigate risks associated with any one particular stream, such as market fluctuations or changes in demand.

In this book, we will explore the top 5 ways to earn passive income. We will delve into the specifics of each method, including how to get started, the pros and cons, and tips for success. By understanding these different methods, you will be able to choose the one that best aligns with your goals, resources, and skills.

Whether you're looking to supplement your current income or create a new stream of income, or set your sights on making your first million dollars, this book will provide you with the knowledge and tools you need to start building your own multi-million dollar passive income business today. From investing in dividend stocks to creating an online courses, the opportunities are endless, and the possibilities are vast. So, let's get started and learn how to make lots of money!

Chapter 1

Explanation of Passive Income

Passive income is a type of income that is earned without the need for active involvement. It is money that is made while you sleep, and it can come from a variety of sources, such as investments, rental properties, and online businesses. The idea behind passive income is to create a source of income that does not require constant attention and effort. This allows for more freedom and flexibility in one's life and the ability to pursue other interests and goals.

One of the key characteristics of passive income is that it is not directly tied to the number of hours worked. Unlike active income, which is earned through a job or self-employment, passive income is not directly tied to the number of hours worked. Instead, it is generated through investments or other activities that require little ongoing effort.

Examples of passive income include:

- Renting out a property
- Investing in dividend-paying stocks
- Investing in mutual funds or exchange-traded funds
- Creating and selling an e-book or online course
- Investing in a business or franchise that generates royalties

Passive income can also come in the form of residual income, which is income that is earned on a recurring basis. This includes royalties from book sales, rental income from properties, and recurring commissions from affiliate marketing.

It's important to note that while passive income is a great way to earn money, it often requires an initial investment of time and money. The key is to find a passive income stream that aligns with your skills, interests, and resources, and to be patient as it takes time for the income to start flowing.

In this book, we will explore the top 5 ways to make passive income. Each chapter will delve into the specifics of each method, including how to get started, the pros and cons, and tips for success. By understanding these different methods, you will be able to choose the one that best aligns with your goals, resources, and skills, and to start building your own passive income.

Chapter 2

Importance of Passive Income

Passive income is a crucial aspect of financial stability and independence. It allows for the generation of income without the need for active involvement and can provide a steady stream of income even when you are not actively working. In this chapter, we will explore the key benefits of passive income and how it can help improve your financial situation.

One of the most significant benefits of passive income is the ability to achieve financial freedom. Passive income streams can provide a source of income that is not tied to a traditional 9-5 job, giving you the freedom to pursue other interests and goals. This can include traveling, starting a family, or pursuing a passion project. Another important benefit is the ability to supplement your active income. Passive income can provide an additional source of income that can help you achieve your financial goals, such as paying off debt, saving for retirement, or investing in real estate. This can help to increase your overall financial stability and security. Passive income can also be an effective way to achieve financial independence. Financial independence is the ability to live off of your passive income streams, without needing to rely on active income. This can provide a sense of security and freedom, as well as the ability to retire early or pursue other opportunities without financial constraints.

Passive income also provides diversification of income streams. Having multiple sources of income can reduce financial risk and better prepare you for unexpected changes in your active income. This can provide a level of financial stability and security that is difficult to achieve through active income alone.

Furthermore, building a successful passive income stream can be incredibly satisfying. It takes time and effort, but the sense of accomplishment that comes with it can be incredibly rewarding.

Chapter 3

Overview of the top 5 proven Principles for Passive Income

Passive income is a type of income that is earned without the need for active involvement. There are many ways to make passive income, but in this chapter, we will focus on the top 5 ways that have proven to be effective and efficient. These methods include:

1. **Investing in dividend-paying stocks:** Investing in stocks that pay dividends can provide a steady stream of passive income. This method is relatively low-risk and can provide a consistent return on investment.

2. **Investing in rental properties:** Rental properties can provide a steady stream of passive income in the form of rent. This method requires an initial investment in a property, but the returns can be substantial over time.

3. **Creating and selling an e-book or online course**: Creating and selling an e-book or online course can provide a steady stream of passive income. This method requires an initial investment of time and effort to create the product, but once created, it can continue to generate income with little to no further effort.

4. **Investing in peer-to-peer lending platforms**: Investing in P2P lending platforms can provide a steady stream of passive income in the form of interest on loans. This method requires an initial investment of capital, but can provide a consistent return on investment with relatively low risk.

5. **Building and monetizing a blog or website**: Building and monetizing a blog or website can provide a steady stream of passive income through advertising, affiliate marketing, and sponsored content. This method requires an initial investment of time and effort to build a following, but can provide substantial returns over time with the right strategy.

Investing in Dividend Stocks

Chapter 4

Definition of Dividend Stocks

Dividend stocks are a type of stock that pays out a portion of the company's earnings to shareholders in the form of dividends. These dividends are usually paid out on a quarterly basis and can provide a steady stream of passive income for investors.

The amount of dividends paid out to shareholders is determined by the company's board of directors and is usually a percentage of the company's earnings. The amount of dividends can vary from year to year and is not guaranteed. However, many companies have a history of consistently paying dividends, making them a reliable source of passive income for investors. When considering investing in dividend stocks, it's important to consider the company's dividend yield. This is the annual dividend payment divided by the stock's price. A higher yield typically indicates a higher return on investment, but it's important to also consider the company's financial health and stability before investing. It's also important to note that dividends are considered taxable income, so it's important to factor in the tax implications when evaluating the potential return on investment.

One of the benefits of investing in dividend stocks is that it allows for the potential for capital appreciation. This means the value of the stock can increase over time, providing the potential for a double return on investment - both from the dividends received and the appreciation of the stock.

Overall, investing in dividend stocks can be a reliable and effective way to make passive income, but it's important to conduct thorough research and consider all factors before making an investment.

Chapter 5

How to invest in dividend stocks

Investing in dividend stocks can be a great way to earn passive income while also potentially growing your overall portfolio value. Here are some key tips to consider when investing in dividend stocks:

1. **Understand the concept of dividends**: A dividend is a payment made by a company to its shareholders, typically on a quarterly basis. Dividend stocks are stocks that pay dividends, as opposed to non-dividend paying stocks.

2. **Look for companies with a history of paying dividends**: Companies that have been paying dividends for a long time are more likely to continue doing so in the future. Look for companies that have a track record of paying and increasing dividends over time.

3. **Consider the dividend yield**: The dividend yield is the annual dividend payment divided by the stock's price. A higher yield generally means a higher income return on your investment, but it's also important to consider the overall health of the company and the sustainability of the dividend.

4. **Research the company**: It's important to research a company before investing in it, and this is especially true for dividend stocks. Look at the company's financials, management, and industry trends to get a sense of its overall health and potential for growth.

5. **Diversify your portfolio**: As with any investment, it's important to diversify your portfolio to spread out risk. Don't put all of your money into one dividend stock, or even one sector or industry. Instead, invest in a mix of companies in different sectors with different dividend yields.

6. **Be prepared for fluctuations**: Dividend stocks, like all stocks, can fluctuate in value. Be prepared for this and don't panic if the value of your dividend stocks drops temporarily.

7. **Re-evaluate your holdings regularly**: It's important to regularly re-evaluate your holdings to ensure that they continue to meet your investment goals. If a company's financials or industry outlook changes, you may need to sell your shares and invest in another company.

By following these tips and doing your research, you can potentially earn a steady stream of income while also potentially growing your overall portfolio value through dividend stock investing.

Chapter 6

Pros and cons of investing in dividend stocks

Investing in dividend stocks can be a great way to earn passive income and potentially grow your overall portfolio value, but it's important to understand the pros and cons before making a decision.

Pros:

1. **Passive income**: One of the main benefits of investing in dividend stocks is the ability to earn passive income through the dividends paid by the company. This can provide a steady stream of cash flow that can be used to supplement your income or reinvested to grow your portfolio.

2. **Potential for growth**: Dividend-paying companies are often more established and financially stable, which can make them a safer investment than non-dividend paying stocks. Additionally, companies that consistently pay and increase their dividends are often growing their earnings, which can lead to an increase in the stock price.

3. **Diversification**: Investing in dividend stocks can also provide diversification for your portfolio, as they can perform differently than other types of investments such as bonds.

Cons:

1. **Limited potential for growth**: While dividend-paying stocks can provide potential for growth, they may not have the same potential for growth as non-dividend paying stocks.

2. **Fluctuation in dividends**: Dividends can fluctuate, and companies may decide to decrease or even eliminate their dividends. This can lead to a decrease in income for the investor and a potential decrease in the stock price.

3. **Higher risk for underperforming**: Dividend stocks can underperform the market during a recession or bear market, as companies may cut or eliminate dividends in order to conserve cash.

4. **Limited options**: Not all companies pay dividends, so the pool of stocks to choose from may be limited.

5. **Tax on dividends**: Dividend income is considered taxable, so investors must be prepared to pay taxes on the dividends they receive.

By understanding the pros and cons of investing in dividend stocks, you can make a more informed decision about whether or not they are the right investment for you. It is always recommended to consult with a financial advisor or do your own research before making any investment decisions.

Chapter 7

Tips for Success

Dividend investing can be a great way to earn passive income and potentially grow your overall portfolio value, but it's important to approach it strategically in order to be successful. Here are some tips for successful dividend investing:

- *Start with a plan*: Before you start investing in dividends, it's important to have a plan in place. This should include your investment goals, risk tolerance, and a plan for diversifying your portfolio.

- *Understand the company*: One of the most important things to consider when investing in dividends is the company behind the stock. Research the company's financials, management, and industry trends to get a sense of its overall health and potential for growth.

- *Look for a track record of consistency*: Companies that have been paying dividends for a long time are more likely to continue doing so in the future. Look for companies that have a track record of paying and increasing dividends over time.

- *Consider the dividend yield*: The dividend yield is the annual dividend payment divided by the stock's price. A higher yield generally means a higher income return on your investment, but it's also important to consider the overall health of the company and the sustainability of the dividend.

- *Diversify your portfolio*: Diversification is key to successful investing, and this is especially true when it comes to dividends. Don't put all of your money into one dividend stock, or even one sector or industry. Instead, invest in a mix of companies in different sectors with different dividend yields.

- *Be patient*: Dividend investing is a long-term strategy. It's important to be patient and not to panic if the value of your dividend stocks drops temporarily. Remember that a fluctuation in value does not necessarily mean a fluctuation in dividends.

- *Monitor your investments regularly*: Keep an eye on your dividend investments and the dividends they pay. If a company's dividends decrease or the company stops paying dividends altogether, it may be time to re-evaluate your investment.

- *Consider reinvesting dividends*: Reinvesting dividends can be a great way to compound your returns over time. This means taking the dividends you receive and using them to purchase additional shares of the same stock, rather than taking the cash. This can help increase your overall dividend income in the long run.

- *Be mindful of taxes*: Dividend income is typically taxed at a higher rate than capital gains, so it's important to be aware of how dividends will impact your overall tax bill. Consider holding dividend-paying stocks in a tax-advantaged account, such as an IRA or 401(k), to reduce the impact of taxes.

- *Stay disciplined*: Dividend investing requires discipline and a long-term perspective. Don't let emotions drive your investment decisions and stick to your plan. Avoid chasing hot stocks or getting caught up in market hype.

In conclusion, dividend investing can be a great way to earn passive income and potentially grow your overall portfolio value. By following these tips and approaching your investments with a long-term perspective, you can increase your chances of success in dividend investing. Remember to always do your own research, consult a financial advisor if needed, and never invest more than you can afford to lose.

Rental Properties

Chapter 8

Overview of Rental Properties

Rental properties, also known as investment properties, are a popular way for individuals to earn passive income and build wealth over time. These properties can take many forms, including single-family homes, apartment buildings, and commercial spaces.

The process of owning a rental property begins with the purchase of the property. Investors can choose to purchase a property outright or with a mortgage, depending on their financial situation. Once the property is acquired, the owner will typically make repairs and upgrades as needed to make the property appealing to potential tenants.

The next step is to find and screen tenants. This process typically includes advertising the property, showing the property to potential tenants, and conducting background and credit checks. Once a tenant is found and has signed a lease, the owner is responsible for collecting rent and managing the property, including handling repairs and maintenance.

Owning a rental property can be a great way to earn passive income, but it also comes with its own set of responsibilities. As a landlord, you are responsible for maintaining the property and ensuring that it is safe and livable for your tenants. You will also need to deal with the occasional problem tenant, eviction, and unexpected repairs.

Despite these challenges, owning rental properties can be a rewarding experience for those who are willing to put in the work. With the right property and the right tenants, rental properties can provide a steady stream of passive income and the potential for significant returns on investment over time.

However, it is important to note that the rental property market can be affected by various factors like interest rates, the overall economy, and local laws and regulations. It is important to do your due diligence and research the market before investing in a rental property. Additionally, it is always recommended to seek professional advice from a real estate agent or financial advisor before making any investment decisions.

Chapter 9

How to Invest in Rental Properties

Investing in rental properties can be a great way to earn passive income and build wealth over time. However, it is important to understand the process and steps involved in order to make informed decisions and be successful as a landlord.

1. **Research the market**: Before making any investment decisions, it is important to research the local real estate market. This includes looking at factors such as median home prices, rental rates, and vacancy rates. Additionally, research on local laws and regulations that may affect your investment.

2. **Create a budget**: Determine how much you can afford to spend on a rental property and create a budget accordingly. This should include the cost of the property, as well as any repairs and upgrades that may be needed.

3. **Find the right property**: Once you have a clear idea of your budget, you can start looking for properties that meet your investment criteria. Consider factors such as location, property type, and potential for return on investment.

4. **Obtain financing**: There are several options for financing a rental property, including a traditional mortgage, a home equity loan, or a private loan. Choose the option that is best for your financial situation and credit score.

5. **Find and screen tenants**: Once the property is acquired and repaired, the next step is to find and screen tenants. This process includes advertising the property, showing the property to potential tenants, and conducting background and credit checks.

6. **Manage the property**: As a landlord, you are responsible for maintaining the property and ensuring that it is safe and livable for your tenants. This includes collecting rent, handling repairs and maintenance, and dealing with problem tenants.

7. **Review and Evaluate**: Regularly review your rental property's financial performance and evaluate whether it is meeting your investment goals.

Investing in rental properties can be a great way to earn passive income and build wealth over time, but it is important to understand the process and steps involved. Additionally, it is recommended to seek professional advice from a real estate agent or financial advisor before making any investment decisions.

It is also important to keep in mind that owning rental properties comes with a certain level of risk and responsibilities, so it's important to be prepared for possible challenges and have a plan to address them.

Chapter 10

Pros and Cons of Investing in Rental Properties

Investing in rental properties can be a great way to earn passive income and build wealth over time, but it is important to understand both the advantages and disadvantages before making a decision.

Pros:

1. **Passive income**: One of the main advantages of owning rental properties is the potential to earn passive income. This means that the property and tenants generate income without the need for active management.

2. **Appreciation**: Over time, the value of real estate can increase, providing potential for significant returns on investment. This can be particularly beneficial for long-term investments.

3. **Tax benefits**: Owning rental properties can provide certain tax benefits, such as deductions for mortgage interest, repairs, and depreciation.

4. **Control**: As a landlord, you have the ability to control the property, including setting rental rates and deciding on repairs and upgrades.

5. **Forced savings**: Investing in rental properties can be a form of forced savings, as the rental income can be used to pay for the mortgage and other expenses associated with the property.

Cons:

1. **Risk**: Investing in rental properties comes with a certain level of risk. The value of the property can decrease, and the property may not generate enough income to cover expenses.

2. **Maintenance and repairs**: As a landlord, you are responsible for maintaining the property and handling repairs. This can be costly and time-consuming.

3. **Tenant issues**: Dealing with problem tenants and evictions can be a significant challenge for landlords.

4. **Responsibilities**: Being a landlord comes with a set of responsibilities, such as ensuring the property is safe and livable for tenants, and dealing with unexpected repairs and maintenance.

5. **Market fluctuations**: The rental property market can be affected by various factors, such as interest rates, the overall economy, and local laws and regulations. This can affect the property's rental income and resale value.

Investing in rental properties can be a great way to earn passive income and build wealth over time, but it is important to understand the advantages and disadvantages before making a decision. It is always recommended to seek professional advice from a real estate agent or financial advisor before making any investment decisions.

Chapter 11

Tips for Successful House Renting

Renting out a house can be a great way to earn passive income, but it also comes with its own set of responsibilities. Here are some tips to help ensure a successful rental experience.

1. *Find the right tenants*: One of the most important factors in successful house renting is finding the right tenants. Screen potential tenants thoroughly by conducting background and credit checks. This will help ensure that you have reliable and responsible tenants who will take good care of your property.

2. *Set fair rent*: It's important to set a fair rent that is in line with the market rate for similar properties in your area. Research comparable properties to determine the going rate and make sure to factor in any additional costs, such as utilities and maintenance.

3. *Keep good records*: Keep accurate and detailed records of all rental income and expenses. This will help you stay organized and ensure that you're able to claim all the tax deductions to which you're entitled.

4. *Communicate effectively*: Communicate clearly and promptly with your tenants regarding any issues or concerns. This will help prevent misunderstandings and build trust and respect.

5. *Be proactive with maintenance*: Regularly inspect the property and address any issues promptly to prevent small problems from becoming big ones. This will not only help keep the property in good condition, but also show your tenants that you care about their well-being.

6. *Be responsive*: Be responsive to your tenant's needs and complaints, and take action quickly to address any issues that arise. This will help to maintain a positive relationship with your tenants and ensure they stay happy and satisfied with their rental experience.

7. *Understand the laws*: Understand the laws and regulations that govern rental properties in your area. This will help you avoid any legal issues and ensure that you're in compliance with all the regulations.

8. *Have a plan for difficult situations*: Have a plan in place for dealing with difficult situations, such as non-payment of rent or eviction. This will help you to handle these situations in a calm and professional manner.

By following these tips, you can help ensure a successful rental experience for both you and your tenants. Remember to always seek professional advice from a real estate agent or legal advisor if you have any questions or concerns.

Peer-to-Peer Lending

Chapter 13

Definition of Peer-to-Peer Lending

Peer-to-peer (P2P) lending is a method of borrowing and lending money without the involvement of traditional financial institutions such as banks. Instead, individuals and businesses can borrow and lend money directly to each other through online platforms, also known as P2P lending platforms. These platforms act as facilitators, connecting borrowers and lenders and handling the administration and management of the loans.

P2P lending emerged as a response to the global financial crisis of 2008, which highlighted the shortcomings of traditional financial institutions and their role in the economic downturn. P2P lending platforms offer an alternative way for borrowers to access credit, and for lenders to earn a return on their investment.

P2P lending can be divided into two main categories: consumer P2P lending and business P2P lending. Consumer P2P lending is when individuals borrow money for personal use, such as paying off debt or funding a home renovation. Business P2P lending is when small businesses and startups borrow money to fund their operations.

One of the key benefits of P2P lending is the potential for higher returns for lenders compared to traditional investments such as savings accounts or bonds. P2P lending platforms typically have lower operating costs than banks, allowing them to offer higher interest rates to lenders. Additionally, P2P lending platforms also offer borrowers access to credit that may not be available through traditional financial institutions.

P2P lending is not without risks, however. Since P2P loans are not backed by any collateral, lenders are at a higher risk of default compared to traditional loans. Additionally, P2P lending platforms are not regulated in the same way as banks, meaning that borrowers may not have the same level of protection.

Overall, P2P lending is a relatively new and rapidly growing industry that offers an alternative way for borrowers and lenders to access credit and earn a return on their investment. While P2P lending is not without risks, it has the potential to disrupt traditional financial institutions and provide greater access to credit for individuals and businesses.

Chapter 2

How to Invest in Peer-to-Peer Lending

Investing in peer-to-peer (P2P) lending can be a great way to earn a higher return on your investment compared to traditional savings accounts or bonds. However, it is important to understand the risks involved and how to properly evaluate potential investments. Before investing in P2P lending, it is important to do your research and understand the different platforms available. Some popular P2P lending platforms include Lending Club, Prosper, and Upstart. Each platform has its own unique features and criteria for borrowers and lenders, so it is important to find one that aligns with your investment goals.

When evaluating potential investments, it is important to consider the creditworthiness of the borrower. P2P lending platforms typically have their own system for evaluating the creditworthiness of borrowers, such as a credit score or income verification. It is also important to consider the loan purpose and the terms of the loan, such as the interest rate and the length of the loan.

It is also important to diversify your investments to minimize risk. Instead of investing a large sum of money into one loan, consider investing smaller amounts into multiple loans. This can help to spread the risk of default across multiple loans, rather than putting all of your investment in one loan.

It is also important to be aware of the fees associated with P2P lending. Some platforms charge origination fees to borrowers and service fees to lenders. It is important to factor in these fees when evaluating potential returns on your investment.

Another important thing to consider is the regulation of the platform you are investing in, as it may vary by country. It's also important to check if the platform is insured or has any protection for the investors in case of a default.

In summary, investing in P2P lending can be a great way to earn a higher return on your investment compared to traditional savings accounts or bonds. However, it is important to understand the risks involved and how to properly evaluate potential investments. It is also essential to diversify your investments, consider the creditworthiness of the borrower, the loan purpose, terms of the loan, and the fees associated with the platform you are investing in.

Chapter 14

Pros and Cons of Investing in Peer-to-Peer Lending

Investing in peer-to-peer (P2P) lending can offer a number of potential benefits and drawbacks. It is important to understand these pros and cons before deciding to invest in P2P lending.

Pros:

1. **High potential returns**: P2P lending platforms typically offer higher interest rates than traditional savings accounts or bonds, which can result in higher returns for investors.

2. **Diversification**: Investing in P2P lending can be a way to diversify your portfolio and spread your risk across multiple loans, rather than putting all of your investment in one stock or bond.

3. **Access to credit**: P2P lending platforms can provide access to credit for borrowers who may not be able to access loans through traditional financial institutions.

4. **Convenience**: Investing in P2P lending can be done online and can be more convenient than traditional investment options such as real estate or stocks.

Cons:

1. **Risk of default**: P2P loans are not backed by any collateral, which means that lenders are at a higher risk of default compared to traditional loans.

2. **Lack of regulation**: P2P lending platforms are not regulated in the same way as banks, which means that investors may not have the same level of protection.

3. **Limited liquidity**: P2P loans are not as easily tradable as stocks or bonds, which means that investors may not be able to quickly sell their investment if they need the money.

4. **Lack of transparency**: P2P lending platforms may not be transparent about the creditworthiness of borrowers, which can make it difficult for investors to evaluate the risk of the loan.

5. **Fees**: Some platforms charge origination fees to borrowers and service fees to lenders, which can reduce the overall returns on investment.

In conclusion, investing in P2P lending can offer a number of potential benefits such as high returns, diversification, and convenience. However, it also poses some risks like default, lack of regulation, limited liquidity, lack of transparency, and fees. It is important to carefully consider these pros and cons before deciding to invest in P2P lending and make sure that it aligns with your investment goals and risk tolerance. It's also important to conduct your own research, understand the platform's policies, regulations, and its protection policies before investing.

Chapter 15

Tips for Successful Peer-to-Peer Lending

Peer-to-peer (P2P) lending can be a great way to earn a higher return on your investment, but it is important to approach it with care and strategy to minimize risks and maximize returns. Here are some tips for successful P2P lending:

1. *Diversify your investments*: Investing in multiple loans, rather than just one, can help to spread the risk of default across multiple loans, rather than putting all of your investment in one loan.

2. *Evaluate the creditworthiness of borrowers*: P2P lending platforms typically have their own system for evaluating the creditworthiness of borrowers, such as a credit score or income verification. It is important to consider these factors when evaluating potential investments.

3. *Understand the loan purpose and terms*: The loan purpose and the terms of the loan, such as the interest rate and the length of the loan, can affect the risk and potential return of the investment.

4. *Research and compare different platforms*: Different P2P lending platforms have different fees, policies, and regulations. It is important to research and compare different platforms to find one that aligns with your investment goals and risk tolerance.

5. *Stay updated with the platform and the loans*: Keep an eye on the performance of the loans you have invested in, monitor the platform's performance and any updates, and be aware of any major changes in the company's policies.

6. *Be prepared for the long-term*: P2P lending is not a get-rich-quick scheme, it's a long-term investment, and it's important to have a long-term investment strategy in place.

7. *Use Automated Investing*: Some platforms offer automated investing options that allow you to set certain criteria for loans you want to invest in, this can save you a lot of time and increase the efficiency of your investment.

In conclusion, P2P lending can be a great way to earn a higher return on your investment, but it is important to approach it with care and strategy. By diversifying your investments, evaluating the creditworthiness of borrowers, understanding the loan purpose and terms, researching and comparing different platforms, staying updated with the platform and the loans, being prepared for the long-term, and using automated investing options, you can minimize risks and maximize returns in your P2P lending investments. Remember to always consult with a financial advisor before making any investment decisions, and to be aware of the risks and regulations associated with P2P lending in your country.

Creating and Selling an E-Course or Online Product

Chapter 16

Overview of e-courses and online products

Selling e-courses and online products has become an increasingly popular business model in recent years. With the rise of the internet and digital technology, it has become easier than ever to create and distribute educational content online.

One of the main advantages of selling e-courses and online products is the potential for significant revenue. E-courses and online products can be sold for a one-time fee or on a subscription basis, providing a steady stream of income for creators. Additionally, the cost of creating and distributing these products is typically lower than traditional in-person courses, which can increase profitability.

Another advantage is the ability to reach a global audience. E-courses and online products can be sold to anyone with an internet connection, regardless of location. This allows creators to target specific markets and niches, and increase their customer base.

However, it's important to note that creating and selling e-courses and online products requires a significant amount of time and effort. It's important to have a clear understanding of your target audience, and to create quality content that will meet their needs. Additionally, it's important to have a solid marketing strategy in place to promote your products and reach potential customers.

One of the most effective ways to sell e-courses and online products is through an online platform, such as a website or marketplace. This allows creators to easily manage their products and track sales, as well as to reach a wider audience. Additionally, there are many e-learning platform providers that allow to sell and distribute the courses, like Teachable, Udemy, Skillshare, and many others.

Another effective way to sell e-courses and online products is through social media, influencer marketing and email marketing. By leveraging these platforms, creators can connect with potential customers and promote their products to a targeted audience.

Overall, selling e-courses and online products can be a profitable business model, but it requires a significant amount of time and effort. By understanding your target audience and creating quality content, as well as having a solid marketing strategy in place, creators can successfully sell their e-courses and online products to a global audience.

Chapter 17

How to create and sell an e-course or online product

Creating and selling an e-course or online product requires a significant amount of planning and effort. However, with the right approach, it can be a profitable and rewarding endeavor.

1. **Identify your target audience**: The first step in creating an e-course or online product is to identify your target audience. This will help you to determine the content and format of your course, as well as to target your marketing efforts.

2. **Develop a course outline**: Once you have identified your target audience, you can begin to develop a course outline. This should include the topics that you will cover, the format of the course, and the estimated length of the course.

3. **Create quality content**: The next step is to create the content for your course. This should be high-quality, informative, and engaging. You can use a variety of mediums, such as video, audio, and text, to create your content.

4. **Promote your course**: Once your course is complete, you will need to promote it to reach potential customers. You can use a variety of marketing techniques, such as social media, influencer marketing, email marketing, and pay-per-click advertising to reach your target audience.

5. **Choose a platform to sell your course**: There are many e-learning platforms like Teachable, Udemy, Skillshare, and many others that allow you to sell and distribute your courses. Choose the one that fits your needs and budget.

6. **Price your course**: Setting a price for your course can be tricky. You want to make sure that you are charging a fair price that reflects the value of your course, but also that it is affordable to your target audience. You can also offer a free trial or a money-back guarantee to help increase conversions.

7. **Monitor and improve**: After your course is launched, it's important to monitor the progress and gather feedback from the students. This will help you to identify areas where you can improve the course and make it more valuable to your target audience.

Creating and selling an e-course or online product is not an easy task, but with the right approach, it can be a profitable and rewarding endeavor. By identifying your target audience, developing a course outline, creating quality content, and promoting your course effectively, you can successfully sell your e-course or online product to a global audience.

Chapter 18

Pros and cons of creating and selling an e-course or online product

Creating and selling an e-course or online product can be a great way to monetize your knowledge and skills. However, it's important to understand both the benefits and drawbacks of this business model before diving in.

Pros:

1. **Potential for significant revenue**: E-courses and online products can be sold for a one-time fee or on a subscription basis, providing a steady stream of income for creators.

2. **Low cost of creating and distributing**: The cost of creating and distributing e-courses and online products is typically lower than traditional in-person courses, which can increase profitability.

3. **Ability to reach a global audience**: E-courses and online products can be sold to anyone with an internet connection, regardless of location, allowing creators to target specific markets and niches and increase their customer base.

4. **Flexibility**: E-courses and online products can be created and sold on the creator's own schedule, and it can be done from anywhere with an internet connection.

Cons:

1. **Time and effort required**: Creating and selling e-courses and online products requires a significant amount of time and effort. It's important to have a clear understanding of your target audience and to create quality content that will meet their needs.

2. **Competition**: The market for e-courses and online products is becoming increasingly crowded, making it more difficult to stand out and attract customers.

3. **Difficulty in reaching potential customers**: Without a solid marketing strategy in place, it can be difficult to reach potential customers and promote your products effectively.

4. **Pricing**: Setting a price for your course can be tricky. You want to make sure that you are charging a fair price that reflects the value of your course, but also that it is affordable to your target audience.

5. **Difficulty in building trust and credibility**: As an e-course or online product creator, you need to build trust and credibility to be able to sell your course. It takes time, effort, and resources to build a reputation as a knowledgeable and reputable expert in your field.

In summary, creating and selling e-courses and online products can be a profitable and rewarding business model, but it's important to understand the pros and cons before diving in. By understanding the time and effort required, the competition in the market, and the difficulty in reaching potential customers, creators can make more informed decisions and increase their chances of success.

Chapter 19

Tips for success selling e-course or online product

Selling e-courses and online products can be a successful business model, but it requires a strategic approach. Here are some tips to help increase your chances of success:

1. *Identify your target audience*: Understanding your target audience is crucial to creating and selling e-courses and online products. Knowing their needs, interests, and pain points will help you to create content that is relevant and valuable to them.

2. *Create high-quality content*: The quality of your e-course or online product is essential to its success. Your content should be informative, engaging, and delivered in a format that is easy to consume.

3. *Build an email list*: Building an email list is an effective way to market your e-course or online product. You can use email marketing to nurture leads and convert them into customers.

4. *Create a landing page*: A landing page is a website page that is designed specifically to convert visitors into leads or customers. It should include a clear call to action, a form to capture contact information, and a description of the benefits of your e-course or online product.

5. *Leverage social media*: Utilizing social media is a powerful way to reach a large audience and promote your e-course or online product. Platforms like Facebook, Twitter, and Instagram can be used to build a following and generate interest in your product.

6. *Offer a free trial or money-back guarantee*: Offering a free trial or money-back guarantee can help increase

conversions by providing potential customers with a low-risk way to try your e-course or online product.

7. *Continuously improve*: Continuously monitor the progress of your e-course or online product, and gather feedback from customers to identify areas for improvement. This will help you to make adjustments and updates to your e-course or online product to ensure that it remains relevant and valuable to your target audience.

8. *Build trust and credibility*: Building trust and credibility with your target audience is essential to sell your course. Share your expertise, be transparent, and engage with your audience.

9. *Choose the right platform*: There are many e-learning platforms like Teachable, Udemy, Skillshare, and many others that allow you to sell and distribute your courses. Choose the one that fits your needs and budget.

10. *Utilize SEO*: Optimizing your e-course or online product website for search engines can help increase visibility and drive more traffic to your site. This can be achieved by incorporating keywords into your website content, meta descriptions, and page titles, as well as building backlinks to your site.

By following these tips, you can increase your chances of success in creating and selling e-courses and online products. Remember that creating and selling e-courses and online products is a process, it takes time and effort but with the right strategy, you can build a successful and profitable business.

Affiliate Marketing

Chapter 20

Definition of affiliate marketing

Affiliate marketing is a type of performance-based marketing in which a business rewards one or more affiliates for each customer or visitor brought about by the affiliate's own marketing efforts.

Affiliates, also known as publishers, partner with businesses to promote their products or services. They do this by promoting the business's products or services through a unique link, known as an affiliate link. When a customer clicks on the affiliate link and makes a purchase, the affiliate earns a commission for the sale.

Affiliate marketing can take many forms, such as content marketing, search engine optimization, pay-per-click advertising, and social media marketing. The key to successful affiliate marketing is finding the right products or services to promote and identifying the target audience that is most likely to be interested in them.

One of the benefits of affiliate marketing is that it allows businesses to reach a wider audience by leveraging the networks and expertise of their affiliates. It also allows businesses to focus on creating and selling products or services, while their affiliates take care of the promotion and sales.

Affiliate marketing can also be a great way for individuals to make money online. Many people have found success as affiliate marketers by promoting products or services that align with their interests or expertise.

However, affiliate marketing also has its challenges. One of the main challenges is the need to constantly identify new products or services to promote and new audiences to target. Additionally, finding the right balance between promoting products and services and providing valuable content to your audience can be a challenge.

In summary, affiliate marketing is a type of performance-based marketing in which a business rewards one or more affiliates for each customer or visitor brought about by the affiliate's own marketing efforts. It can be a great way for businesses to reach a wider audience and for individuals to make money online, but it also requires a strategic approach and the ability to constantly adapt to changing market conditions.

Chapter 21

How to get started with affiliate marketing

Getting started with affiliate marketing can seem daunting, but it is a relatively straightforward process once you understand the basics. Here are the steps you can take to get started with affiliate marketing:

1. **Identify a niche**: The first step in getting started with affiliate marketing is to identify a niche or industry that you are passionate about or have knowledge of. This will make it easier for you to find products or services to promote and to connect with potential customers.

2. **Research affiliate programs**: Once you have identified your niche, research affiliate programs that are available in that niche. Look for programs that offer products or services that align with your interests and that have a good reputation.

3. **Sign up for an affiliate program**: Once you have found a program that interests you, sign up to become an affiliate. This will typically involve filling out an application and providing some basic information about yourself and your website or blog.

4. **Get your affiliate link**: After you have been approved as an affiliate, you will be provided with a unique affiliate link. This link is what you will use to promote the products or services of the business you are affiliated with.

5. **Start promoting**: Once you have your affiliate link, you can start promoting the products or services of the business you are affiliated with. You can do this through a variety of channels, such as your website or blog, social media, email marketing, and pay-per-click advertising.

6. **Monitor your progress**: Be sure to monitor your progress as an affiliate marketer. Keep track of your click-through rates, conversion rates, and commission earnings. Use this information to make adjustments to your strategy and improve your performance.

7. **Network and Learn**: Network with other affiliate marketers and learn from their strategies, successes, and mistakes. Join affiliate marketing communities, attend webinars, read articles and blogs, and take online courses to improve your skills and knowledge.

8. **Stay compliant**: Make sure you are aware of the Federal Trade Commission (FTC) guidelines for affiliate marketing and stay compliant with them. Be transparent about your affiliations and disclose any sponsored posts or reviews.

By following these steps, you can get started with affiliate marketing and start earning commissions by promoting products and services that align with your interests and expertise. Remember that affiliate marketing is a process and it takes time and effort to be successful. But with the right strategy and persistence, you can build a profitable affiliate marketing business.

Chapter 22

Pros and cons of affiliate marketing

Affiliate marketing can be a great way for businesses to expand their reach and for individuals to earn money online. However, like any business model, it has its pros and cons.

Pros of Affiliate Marketing:

1. **Low barrier to entry**: Affiliate marketing has a relatively low barrier to entry, meaning that anyone can start an affiliate marketing business with minimal investment.

2. **Flexibility**: Affiliate marketing allows for a great deal of flexibility in terms of when and where you work. This makes it a great option for those who want to work from home or have a flexible schedule.

3. **Unlimited earning potential**: There is no limit to how much you can earn through affiliate marketing. The more effort you put into promoting products and services, the more you can earn.

4. **No customer service**: As an affiliate marketer, you are not responsible for customer service, refunds, or returns. This means you can focus on promoting products and services rather than dealing with customer complaints.

5. **Low overhead costs**: Affiliate marketing has low overhead costs, as there is no need to invest in inventory or physical goods. This makes it a great option for those who want to start a business with minimal investment.

Cons of Affiliate Marketing:

1. **No guaranteed income**: There is no guarantee of income in affiliate marketing. It can take time to establish a successful affiliate marketing business and there is no guarantee that you will earn a certain amount of money.

2. **Increased competition**: Affiliate marketing has become more popular over time, which has led to increased competition. This can make it more difficult to establish a successful affiliate marketing business.

3. **No control over products or services**: As an affiliate marketer, you have no control over the products or services you are promoting. This means that you have no say in the pricing, quality, or availability of the products or services you are promoting.

4. **Need to constantly find new products and services**: Affiliate marketing requires that you constantly find new products and services to promote. This can take a lot of time and effort.

5. **Compliance**: As an affiliate marketer, you are responsible for staying compliant with Federal Trade Commission (FTC) guidelines and laws. This can be a challenge, especially for those who are new to affiliate marketing.

Overall, affiliate marketing can be a great way to earn money online and grow a business, but it also has its challenges. It is important to consider both the pros and cons before starting an affiliate marketing business and make sure that you have a solid plan in place to succeed.

Chapter 23

Tips For Successful Affiliate Marketing

Affiliate marketing can be a great way to earn money online, but it also requires a strategic approach and the ability to constantly adapt to changing market conditions. Here are some tips for being successful with affiliate marketing:

1. *Choose the right niche*: The first step in being successful with affiliate marketing is to choose the right niche. This means finding a niche or industry that you are passionate about or have knowledge of. This will make it easier for you to find products or services to promote and to connect with potential customers.

2. *Choose the right affiliate programs*: Choose affiliate programs that offer products or services that align with your interests and that have a good reputation. Carefully read the terms and conditions of the program, and make sure that you understand the commission structure.

3. *Build a website or blog*: Building a website or blog is an effective way to promote products and services as an affiliate marketer. This will give you a platform to share your thoughts and reviews, and to connect with potential customers.

4. *Optimize your website or blog*: Optimize your website or blog for search engines by using keywords in your content, meta tags, and URLs. This will help potential customers find your website or blog when they search for products or services that you promote.

5. *Use social media*: Use social media to connect with potential customers and to promote products or services. Platforms like Facebook, Twitter, and Instagram can be great places to share your thoughts, reviews, and affiliate links.

6. *Utilize email marketing*: Use email marketing to connect with potential customers and promote products or services. Build an email list of subscribers who have opted-in to receive your emails, and use it to promote affiliate products or services.

7. *Monitor your progress*: Keep track of your click-through rates, conversion rates, and commission earnings. Use this information to make adjustments to your strategy and improve your performance.

8. *Be transparent*: Be transparent about your affiliations and disclose any sponsored posts or reviews. This will build trust with your audience, and it's also a requirement of the Federal Trade Commission (FTC) guidelines for affiliate marketing.

9. *Network and learn*: Network with other affiliate marketers and learn from their strategies, successes, and mistakes. Join affiliate marketing communities, attend webinars, read articles and blogs, and take online courses to improve your skills and knowledge.

10. *Constantly adapt*: Affiliate marketing is a constantly changing industry, so it's important to stay up-to-date with the latest trends and strategies. Be open to trying new things, and be willing to pivot your strategy if something isn't working.

By following these tips, you can increase your chances of success in affiliate marketing and build a profitable business promoting products and services that align with your interests and expertise.

Conclusion

Passive income is a valuable tool for achieving financial freedom and security. By creating streams of income that require minimal effort to maintain, individuals can free up time and energy to pursue other goals and interests. Passive income can come in many forms as described in this book, such as rental properties, investments, and online businesses.

However, it is important to note that creating passive income streams takes time and effort upfront. Investing in real estate, for example, requires a significant amount of money and research to find profitable properties. Building an online business also requires a significant amount of time and effort to create and market a product or service.

It is also important to be aware of the potential risks associated with passive income streams, such as market fluctuations and changes in demand for a particular product or service. Diversifying one's income streams can help mitigate these risks.

In conclusion, becoming a millionaire through passive income streams is possible but requires a significant amount of planning, effort, and investment.

Building a diversified portfolio of income streams can help mitigate the risks associated with any one particular stream and increase the chances of achieving financial freedom and security.

And as always, it is important to consult with a financial advisor before making any significant financial decisions.

Chapter 24

A Few More Resources

Here are a few resources that can provide additional information on passive income and how to generate it:

1. **Bankrate**: This website offers a variety of financial advice, including information on passive income. They have a survey on passive income which can be found here: https://www.bankrate.com/banking/savings/survey-shows-who-has-passive-income-and-how-they-use-it/

2. **National Association of Realtors**: The NAR conducts research on various aspects of the real estate market, including rental properties. Their study on rental properties can be found here: https://www.nar.realtor/research-and-statistics/research-reports/investment-and-vacation-home-buyers-survey

3. **Economic Policy Institute**: This think tank conducts research on economic policy, including the distribution of wealth and income. Their study on the distribution of stocks can be found here: https://www.epi.org/publication/the-wealthy-handful-who-own-americas-stock-market-hold-an-ever-larger-share-of-it/

4. **Small Business Administration**: The SBA provides resources and support for small businesses, including information on business ownership and passive income. Their study on small business ownership can be found here: https://www.sba.gov/sites/default/files/advocacy/2020-Small-Business-Profiles-US.pdf

5. **National Women's Business Council**: This council conducts research on women-owned businesses and provides recommendations for policies that support their growth. Their study on women-owned businesses and passive income can be found here: https://www.nwbc.gov/research/women-owned-businesses-passive-income

6. **National Community Reinvestment Coalition**: This organization works to promote access to credit and investment in underserved communities. Their study on minority-owned businesses and passive income can be found here: https://www.ncrc.org/wp-content/uploads/2019/03/NCRC-Minority-Business-Report-2019.pdf

Chapter 25

They Make Millions!

Many successful and famous people have built passive income streams through investments, rental properties, and businesses that require minimal ongoing effort to maintain. In this chapter, we will take a look at some of the famous people who have built significant passive income streams.

1. Warren Buffett

Warren Buffett, often considered the greatest investor of all time, is a master at building passive income through investments. He is the chairman and largest shareholder of Berkshire Hathaway, a conglomerate that owns a wide range of businesses, including insurance, energy, and retail companies. By holding shares in these companies, Buffett earns passive income through dividends and capital gains.

2. **Oprah Winfrey**

Oprah Winfrey, the media mogul, has built a significant passive income stream through her production company, Harpo Productions. Harpo Productions has produced a number of successful shows, including "The Oprah Winfrey Show," "Dr. Phil," and "Rachael Ray." By owning the rights to these shows, Oprah earns passive income through royalties and syndication fees.

3. **Robert Kiyosaki**

Robert Kiyosaki, the author of the bestselling book "Rich Dad, Poor Dad," is a strong advocate of building passive income through real estate investments. He has built a significant passive income stream through rental properties, as well as through his real estate investment company, Rich Global LLC.

4. **Tony Robbins**

Tony Robbins, the motivational speaker and personal development coach, has built a significant passive income stream through his personal development products and programs. By creating products such as books, CDs, and online courses, Robbins earns passive income through royalties and licensing fees.

5. **J.K. Rowling**

J.K. Rowling, the author of the Harry Potter series, has built a significant passive income stream through her books, movies, and merchandise. By owning the rights to the Harry Potter franchise, Rowling earns passive income through royalties, licensing fees, and merchandise sales.

6. **Mark Zuckerberg**

Mark Zuckerberg, the founder of Facebook, has built a significant passive income stream through his ownership stake in the company. As the majority shareholder of Facebook, Zuckerberg earns passive income through dividends and capital gains.

These famous people have built significant passive income streams through a variety of means, including investments, rental properties, and businesses that require minimal ongoing effort to maintain. By understanding how they have built their passive income streams, you can gain valuable insights into the strategies and tactics that can be used to build your own path to success and financial freedom.

Chapter 26

Next Steps

In the previous chapter, we looked at some famous people who have built significant passive income streams. Now, let's explore some steps that can be taken to implement passive income strategies in your own life.

1. Understand your current financial situation: Before you can start building passive income streams, it's important to have a clear understanding of your current financial situation. This includes your income, expenses, assets, and liabilities. By understanding your current financial situation, you can identify areas where you can cut costs and free up capital to invest in passive income strategies.

2. Set clear financial goals: Once you have a clear understanding of your current financial situation, it's important to set clear financial goals. These goals should be specific, measurable, and achievable. Examples of financial goals may include saving a certain amount of money, paying off a certain amount of debt, or investing in a certain number of rental properties.

3. Research different passive income strategies: There are many different passive income strategies to choose from as described in this book. It's important to fully research the different strategies and find one that aligns with your financial goals and risk tolerance.

4. Create a plan and take action: Once you have chosen a passive income strategy, it's important to create a plan and take action. This includes researching the market, identifying opportunities, and making investments.

5. Keep track of your progress: It's important to keep track of your progress and adjust your plan as needed. This includes monitoring your investments and rental properties, analyzing your cash flow, and adjusting your budget as needed.

6. Diversify: Diversification is key to building a robust passive income stream. By diversifying your investments and income streams, you reduce the risk of losing all your income in case one of the streams fail.

7. Seek Professional help: If you are new to passive income strategies, it can be helpful to seek professional help. Financial advisers, accountants, and attorneys can provide valuable advice on creating a plan, identifying opportunities, and minimizing risks.

Chapter 27

Road to Success

The road to success is not always easy, but with hard work, dedication, and a clear plan, you can achieve your financial goals.

As you embark on this journey, it is important to remember that there will be challenges and setbacks along the way. However, it is important to not let these setbacks discourage you. Instead, use them as learning opportunities and adjust your plan as needed.

One of the keys to success is to stay focused on your goals, and to remind yourself of why you started on this journey in the first place.

It can be helpful to write down your goals and place them somewhere where you can see them every day.

Another important aspect of success is to surround yourself with positive and supportive people. Having a support system can provide encouragement and motivation when you need it most. Seek out people who have experience and knowledge in the areas you are trying to succeed in, they can be great mentors and guides.

Remember that building passive income streams takes time and patience. Don't expect overnight success. Be consistent in your efforts, and trust that your hard work will pay off in the long run.

Finally, it's important to remember that success is not just about money and financial gain. True success is about living a fulfilling and balanced life, where you have the freedom and flexibility to pursue your passions and interests. May your efforts be rewarded with financial freedom and the ability to live the life you have always dreamed of.

* 9 7 9 8 3 7 5 2 0 8 2 3 7 *